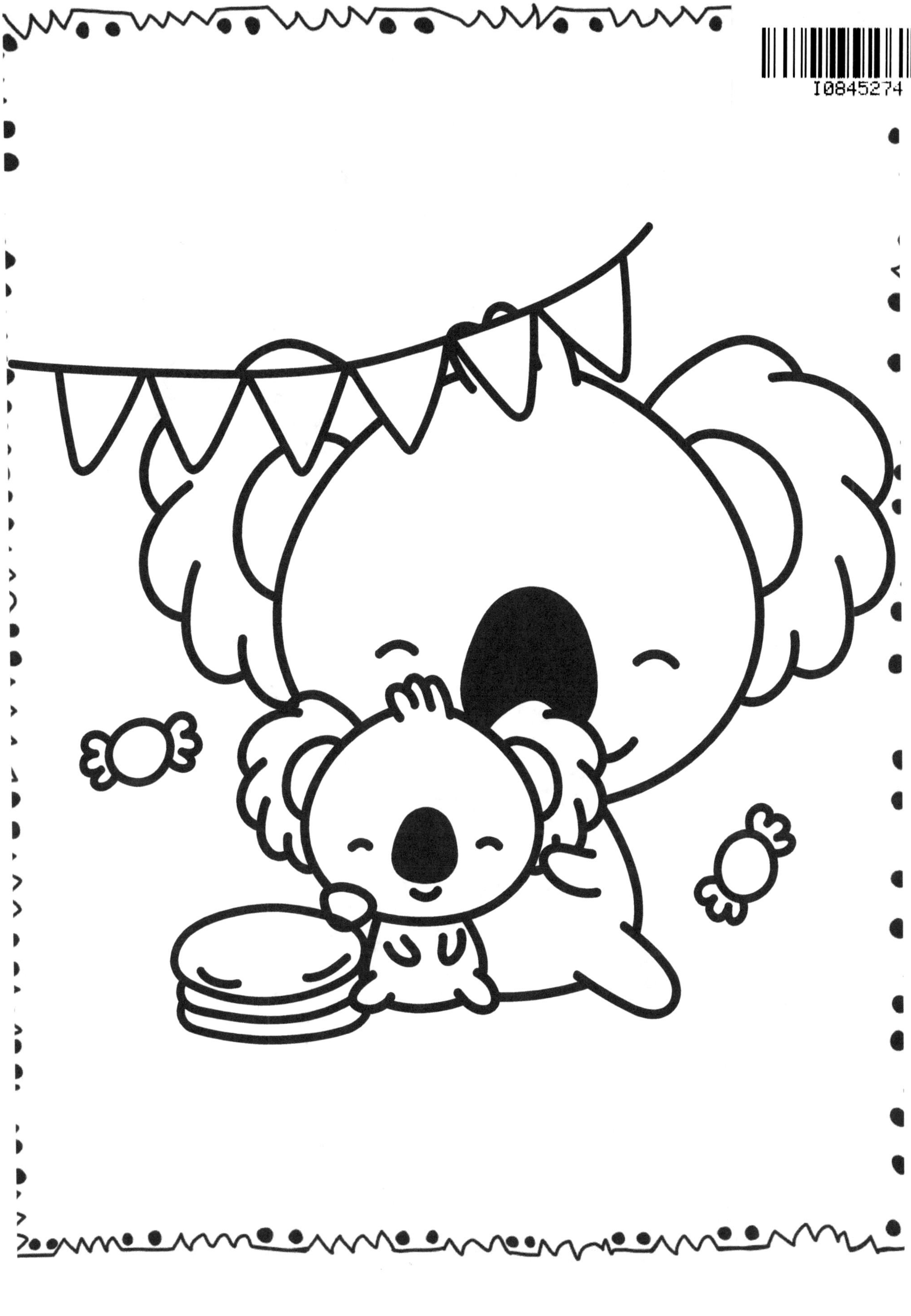

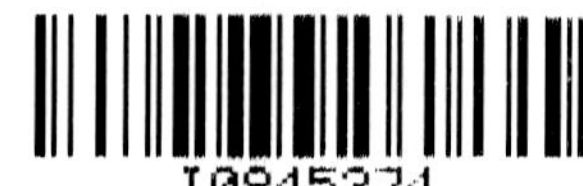

I0845274

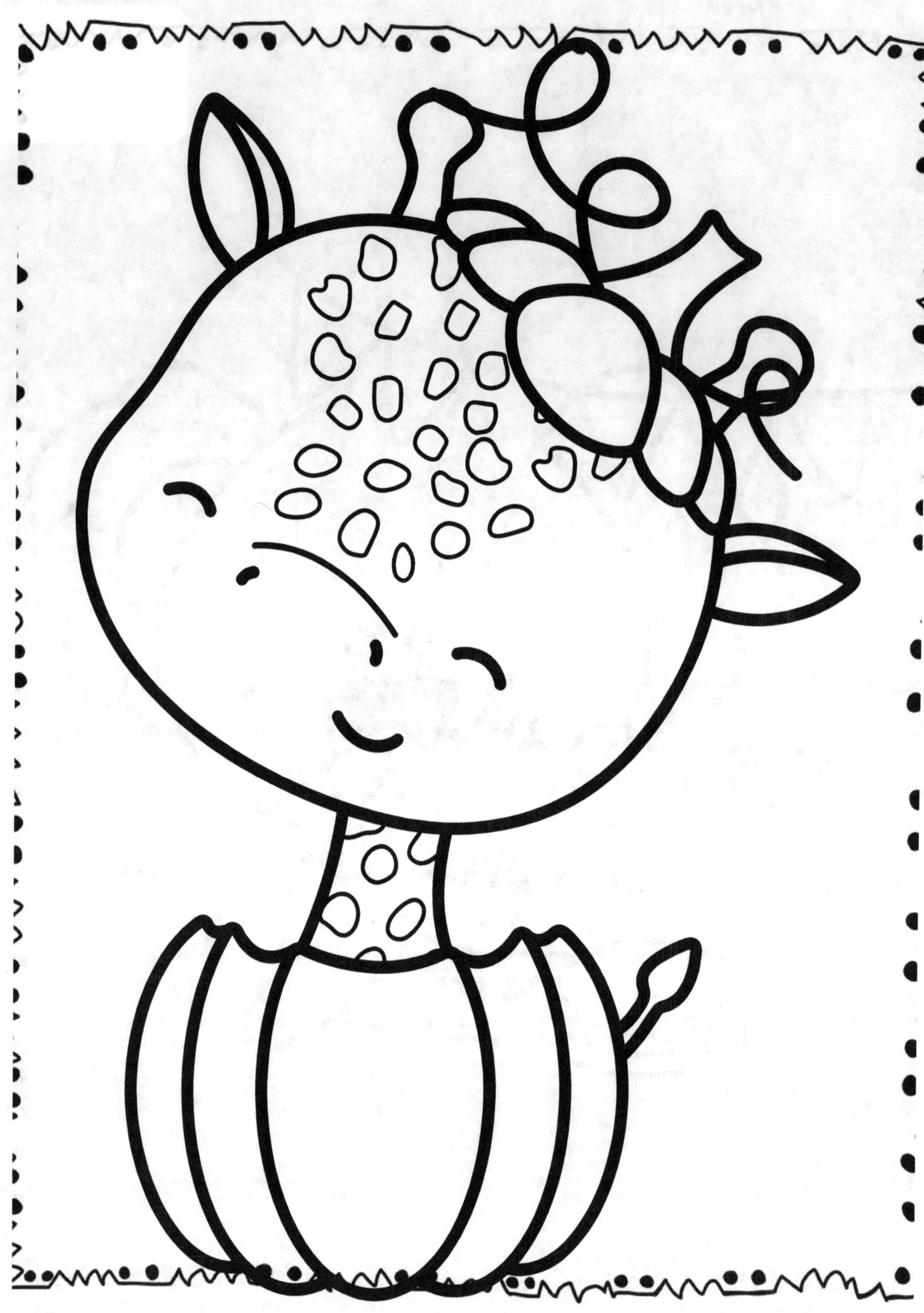

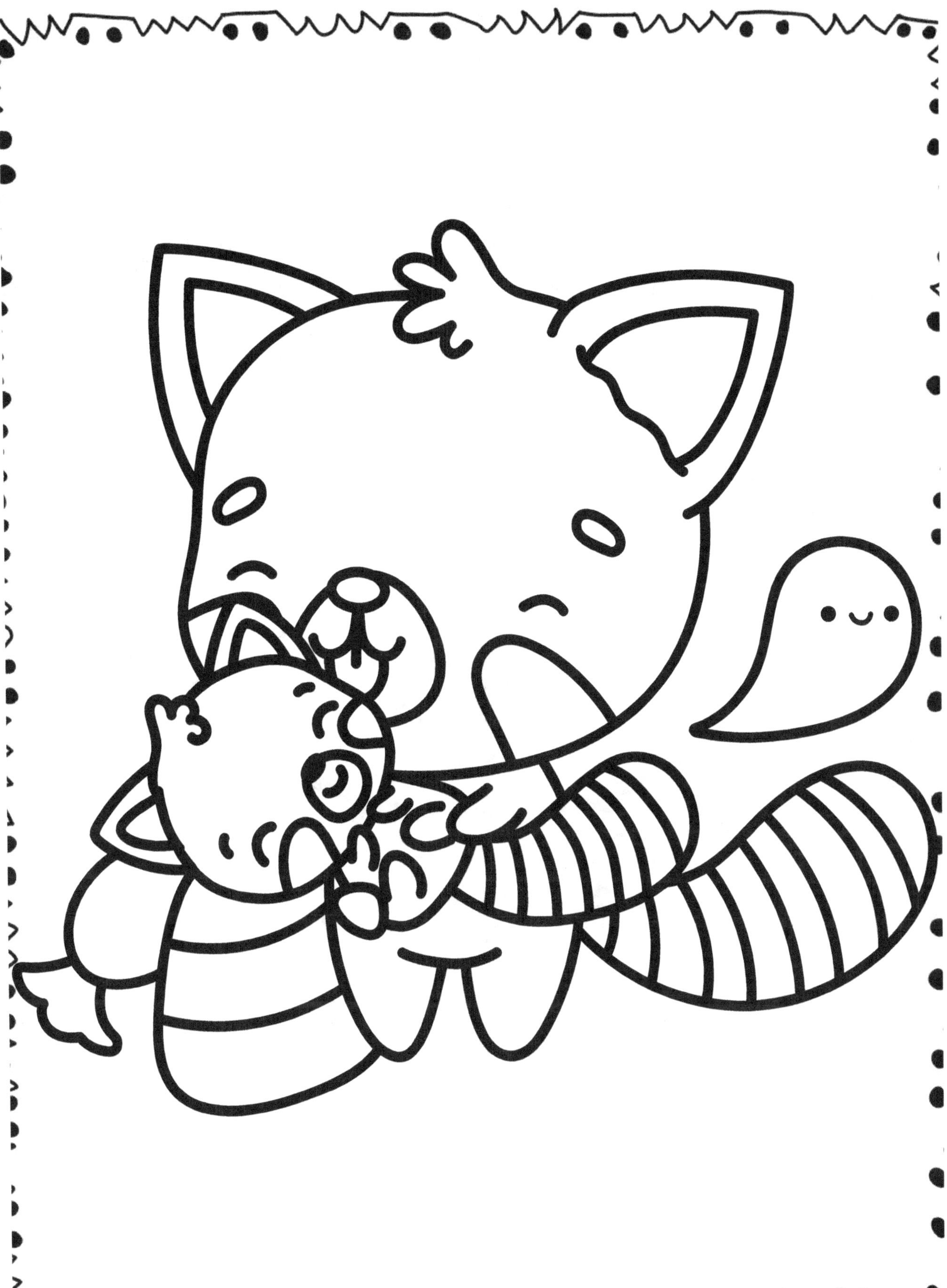

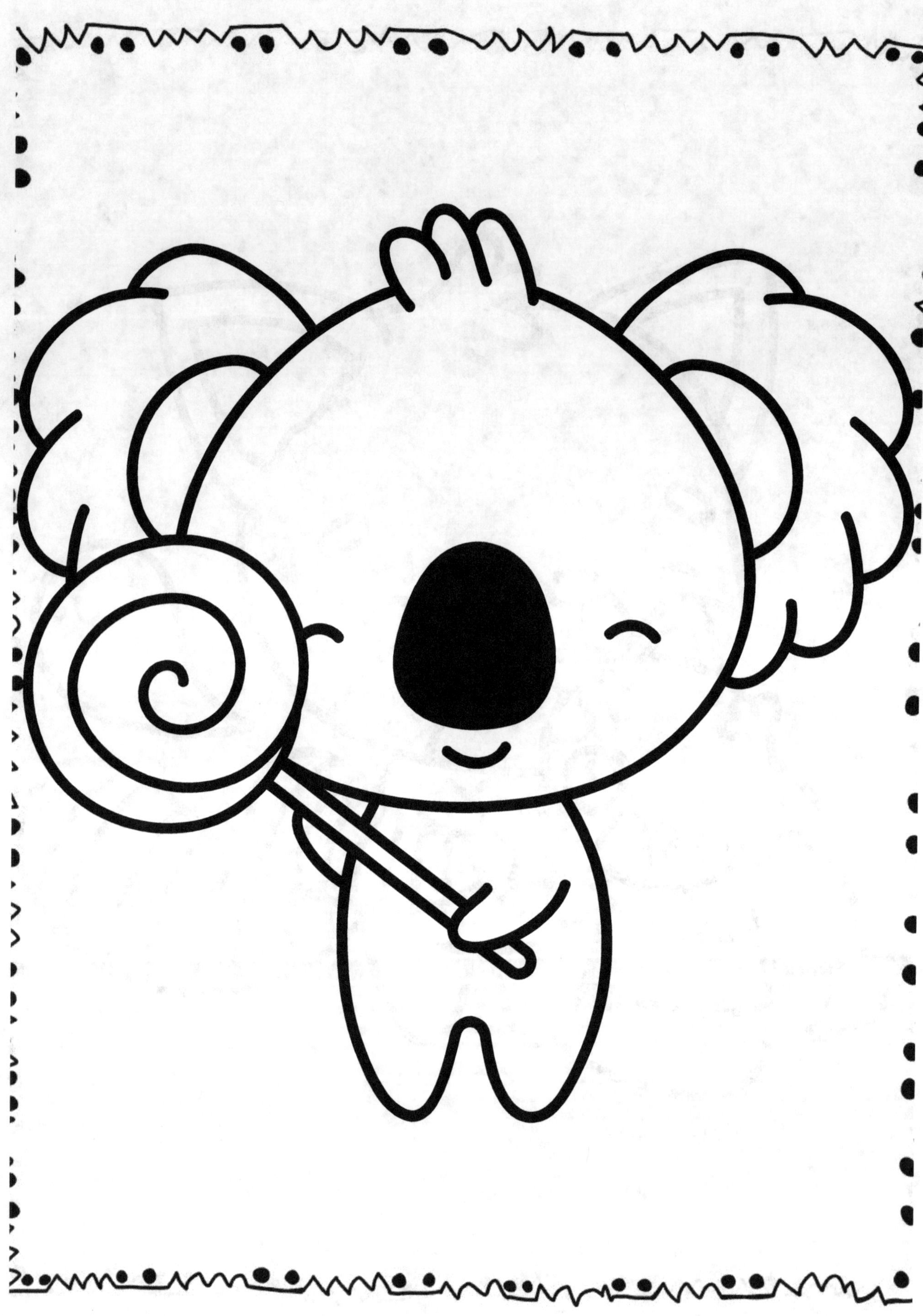

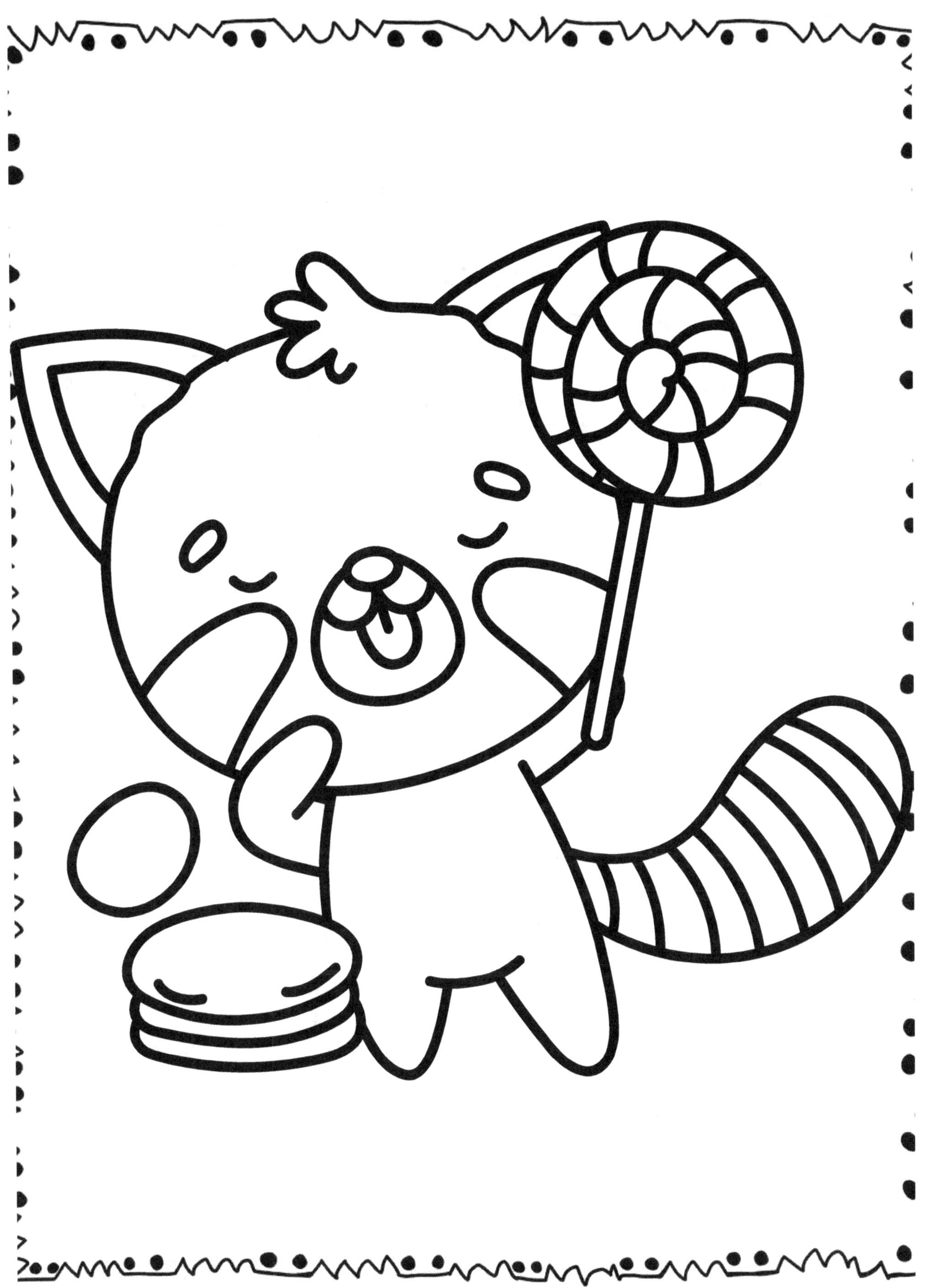

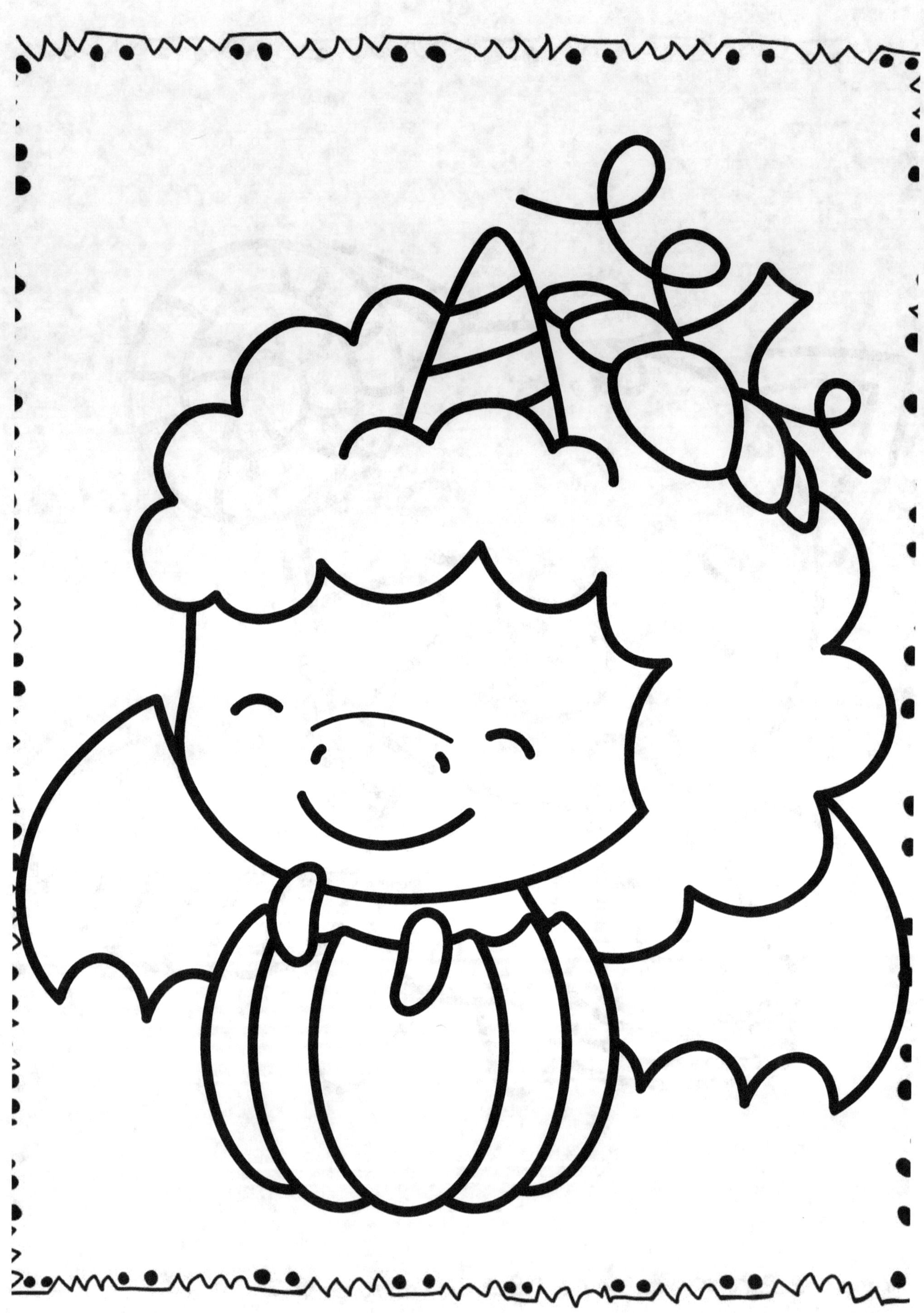

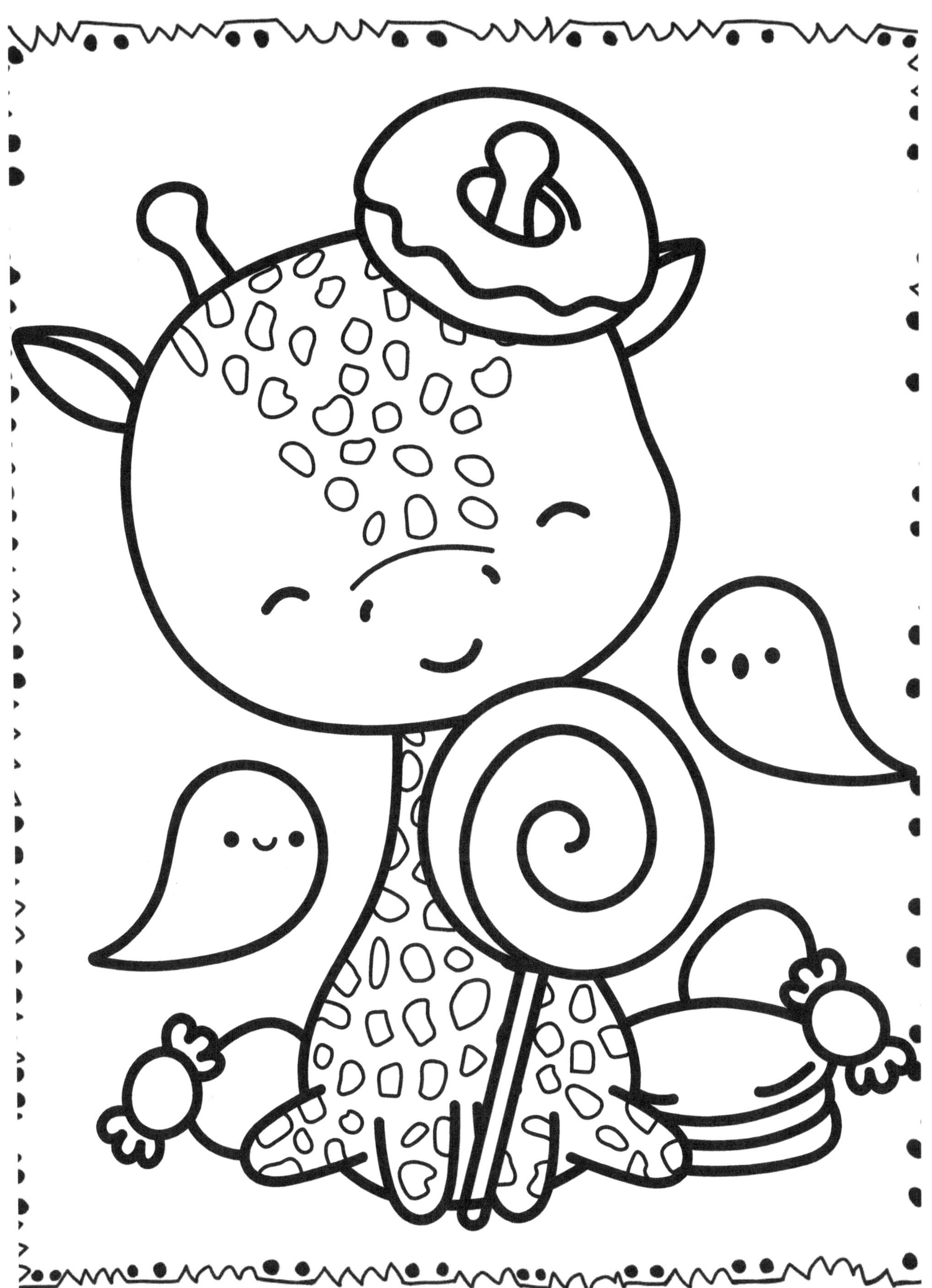

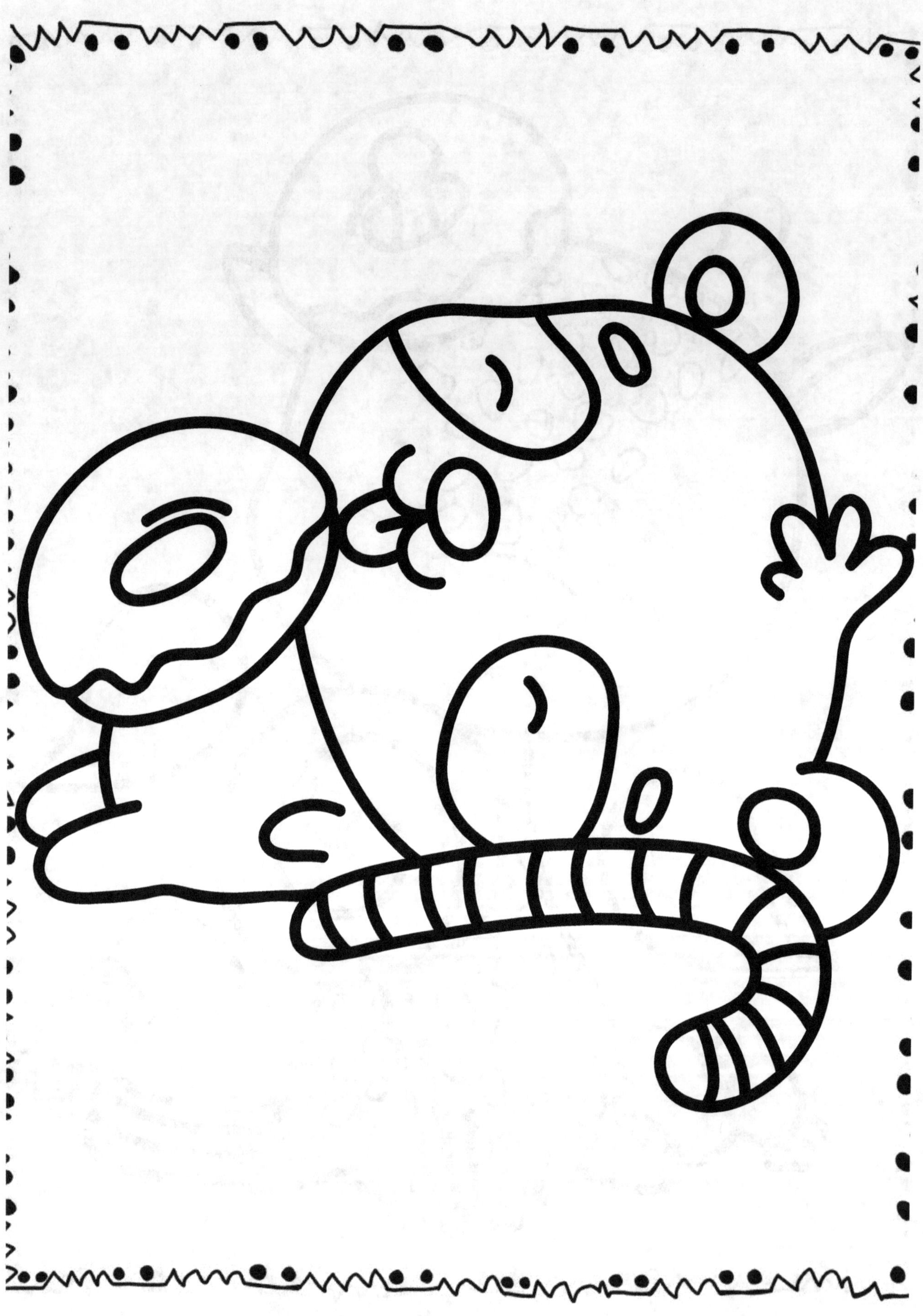

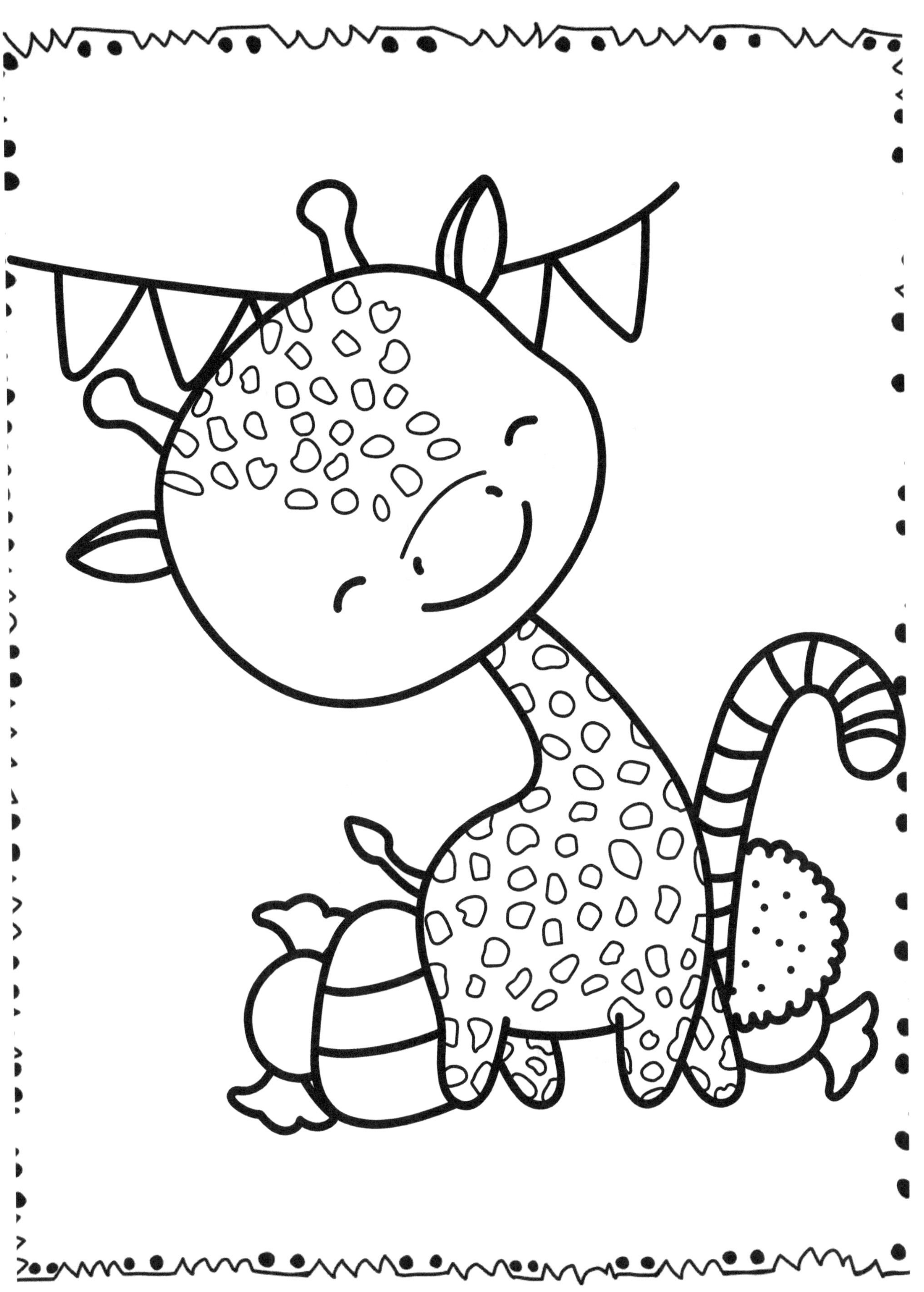

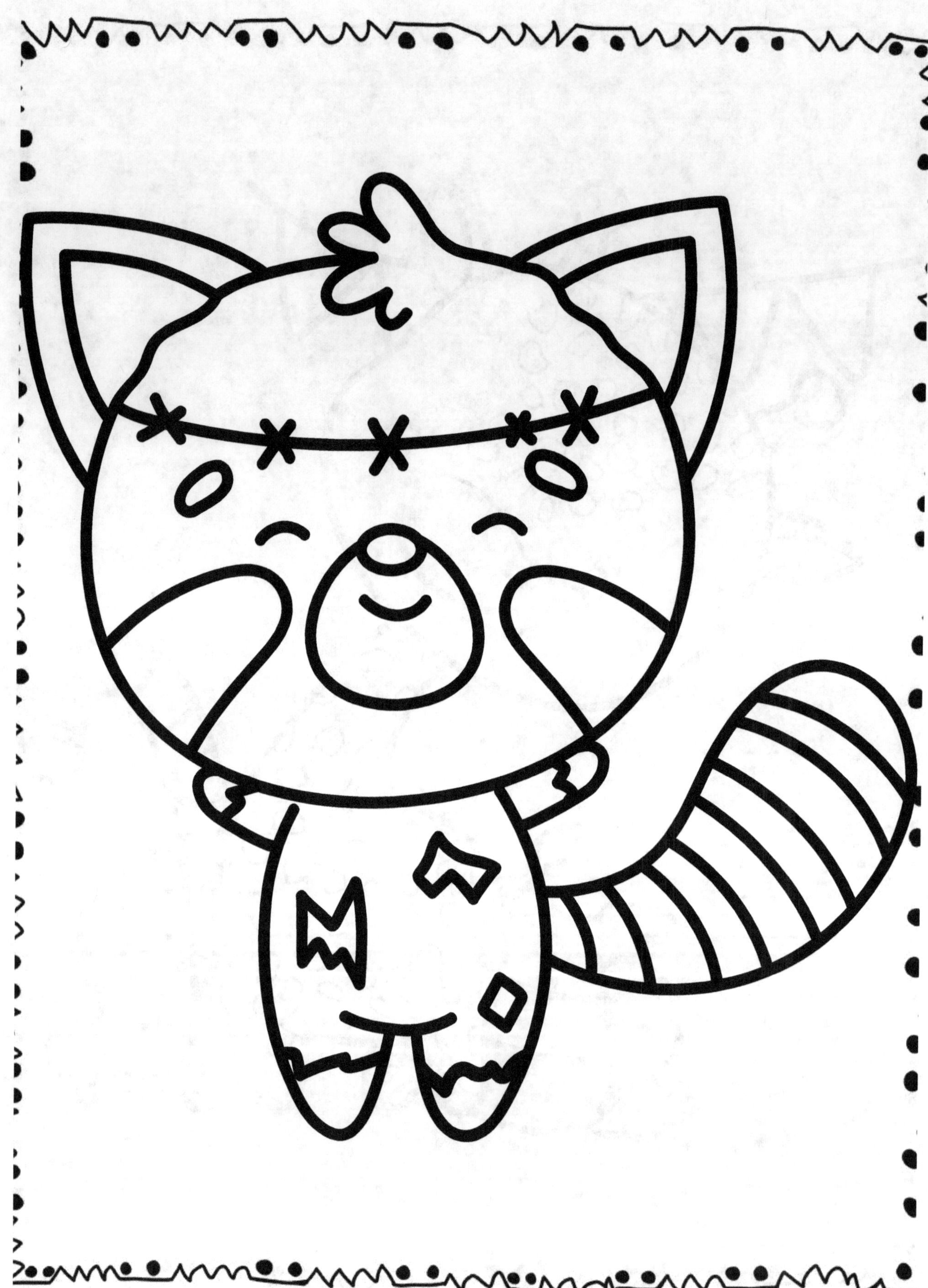

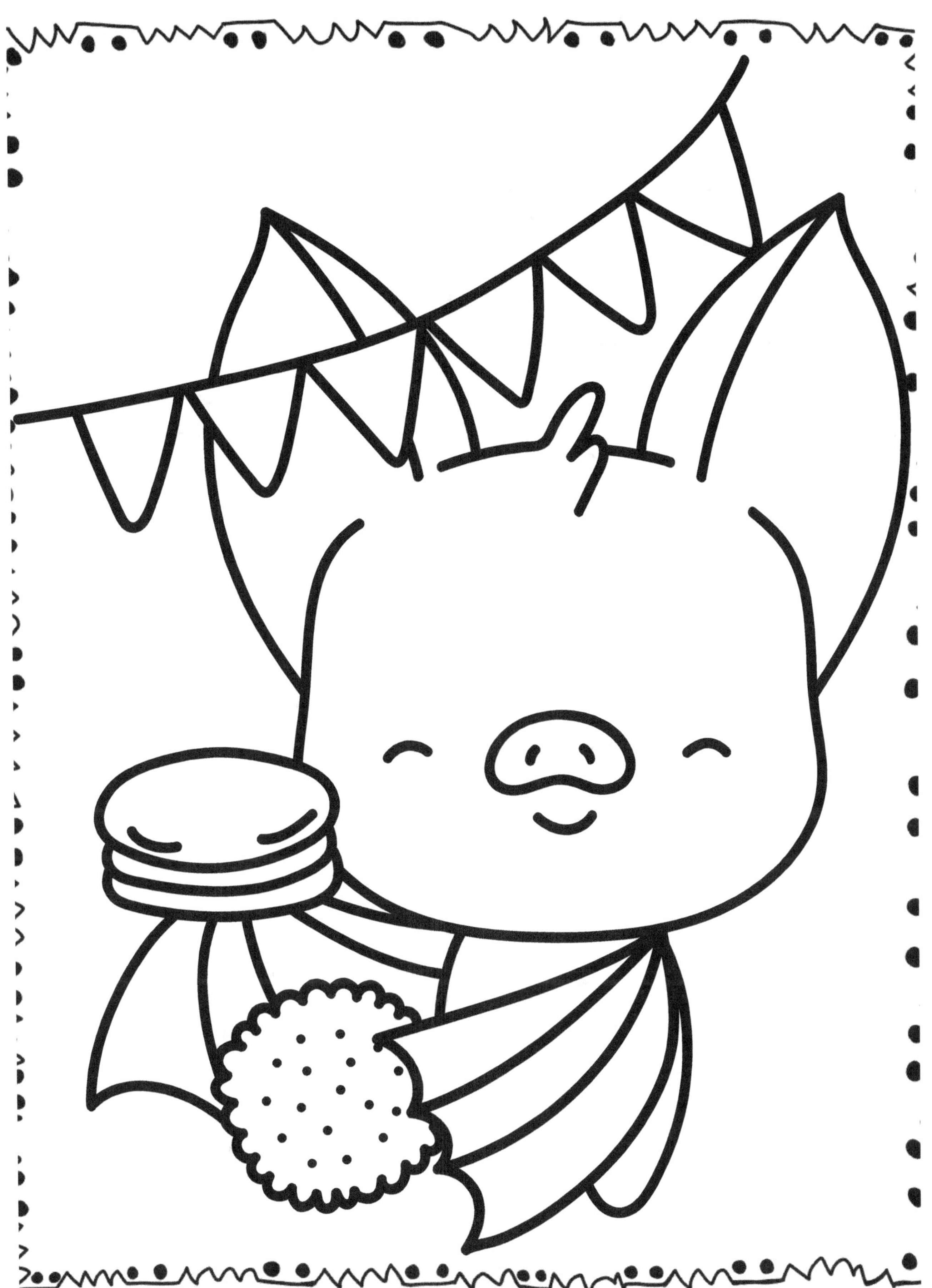

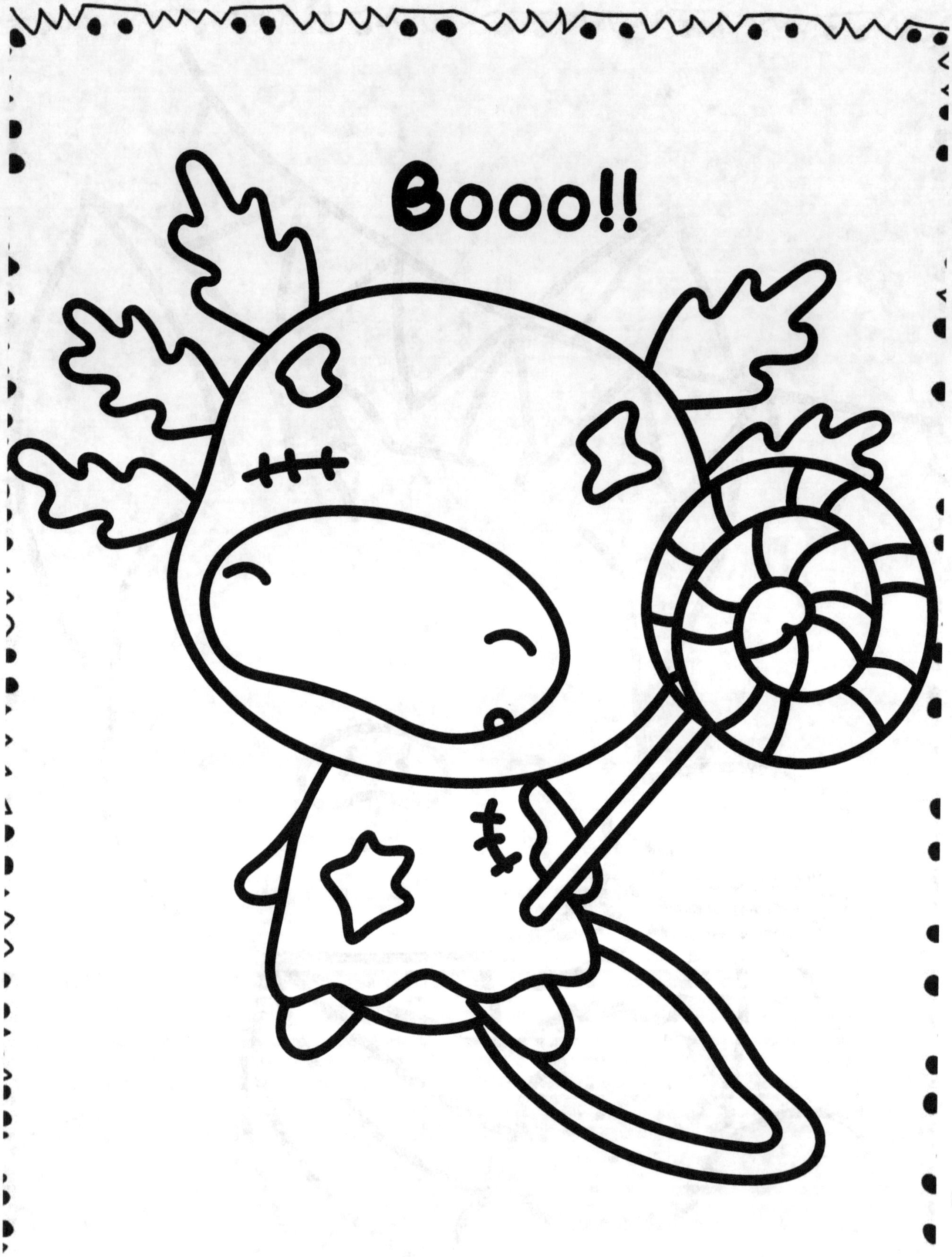

Booo!!

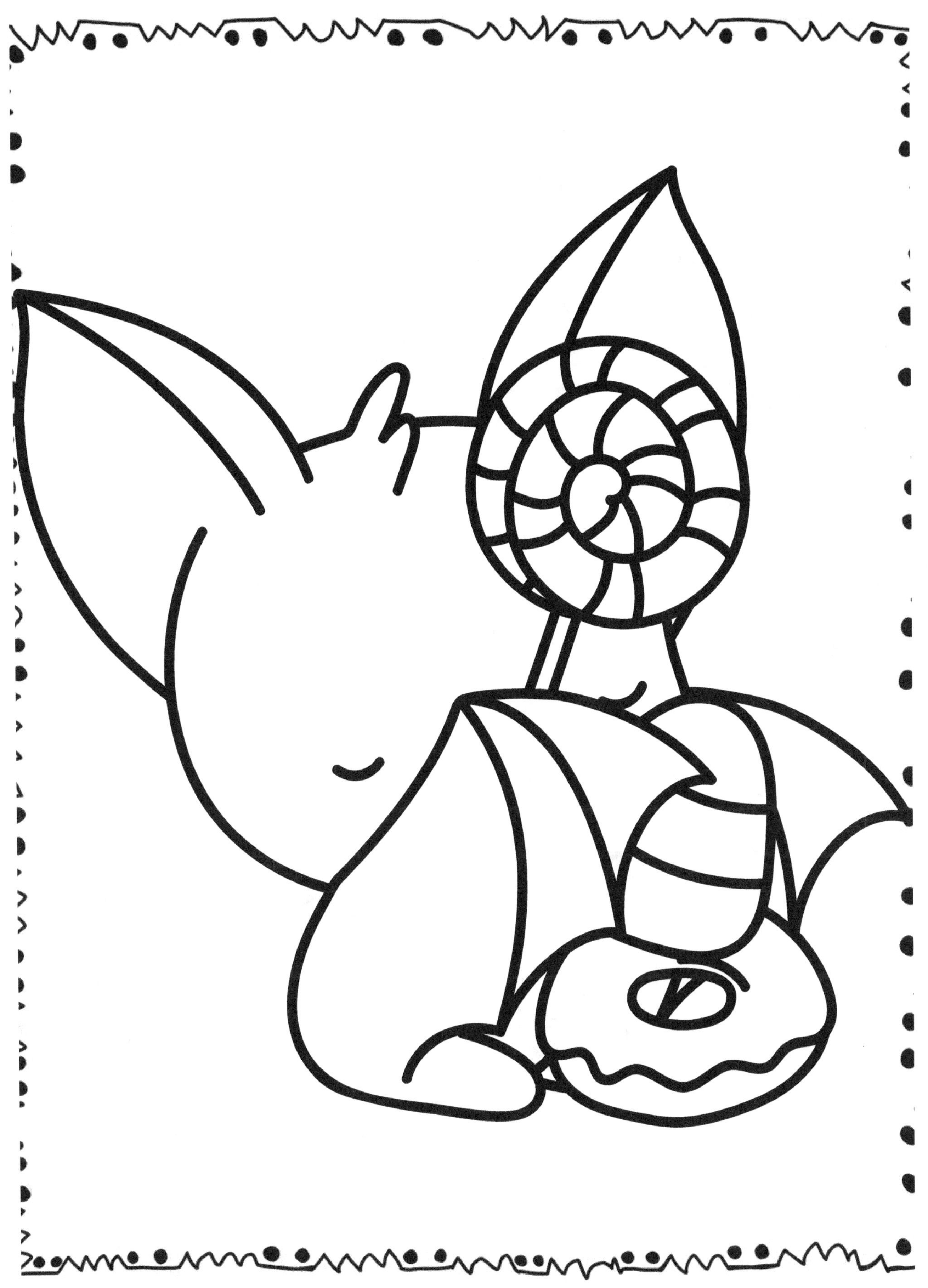

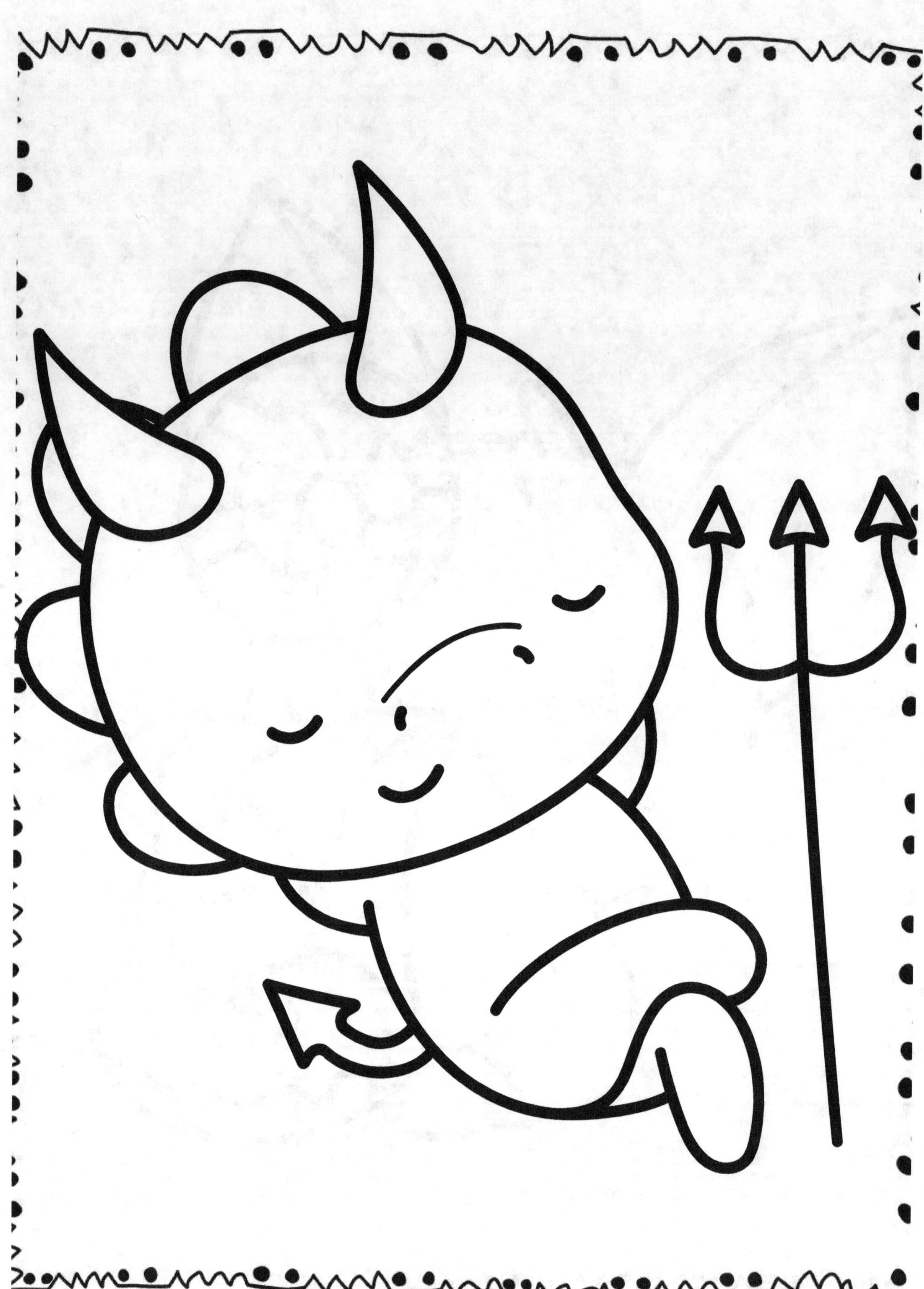

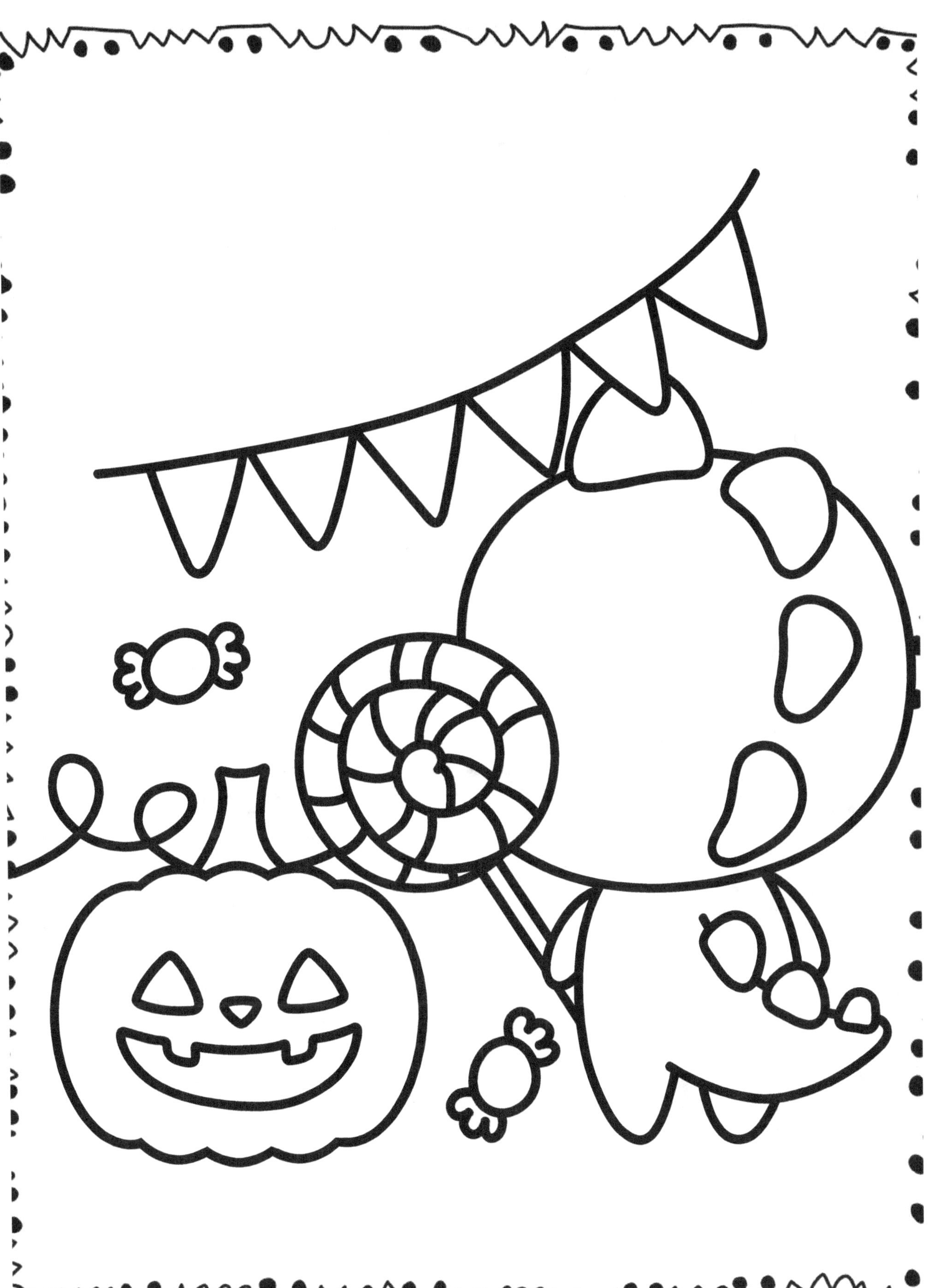

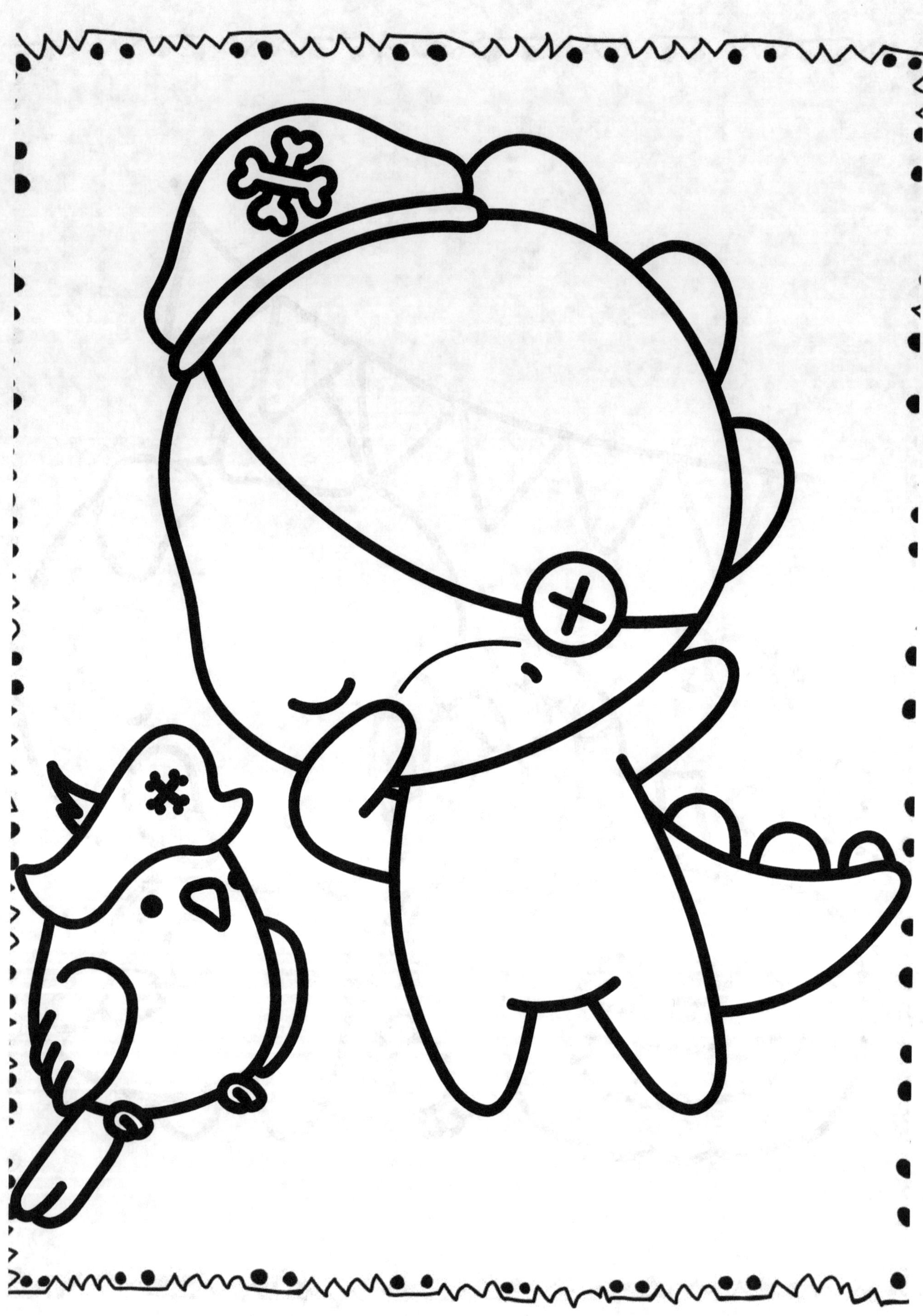

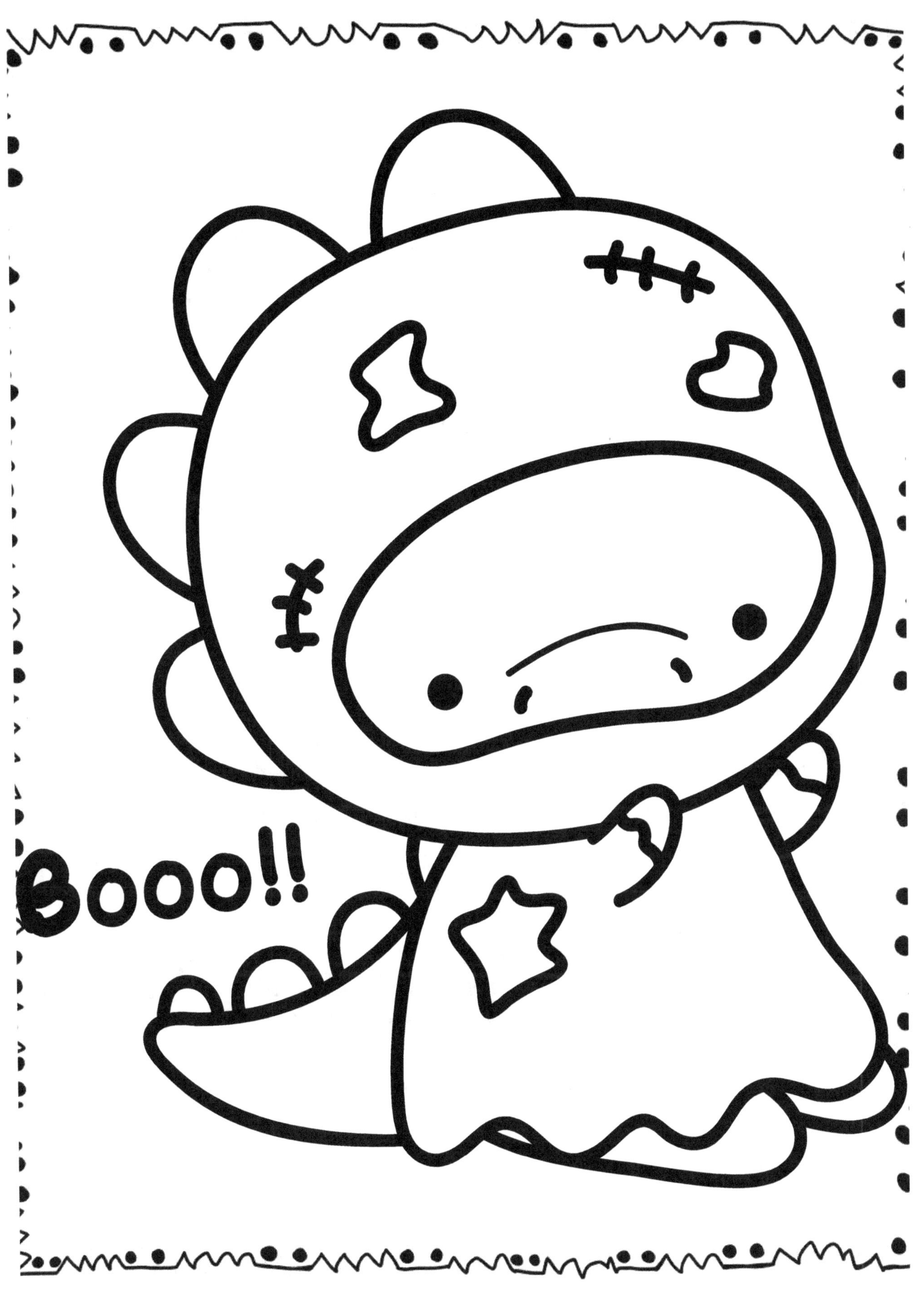
Booo!!

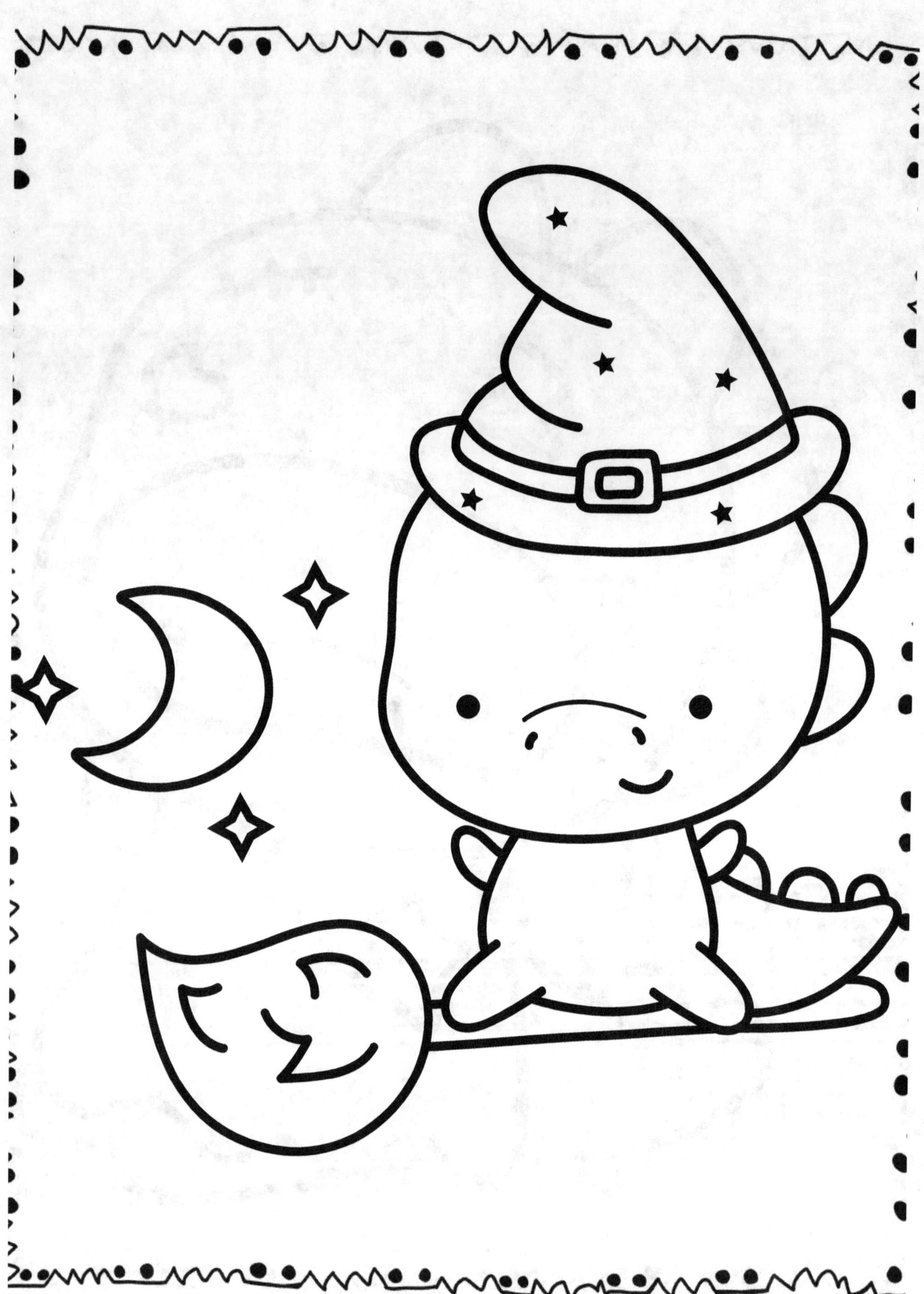

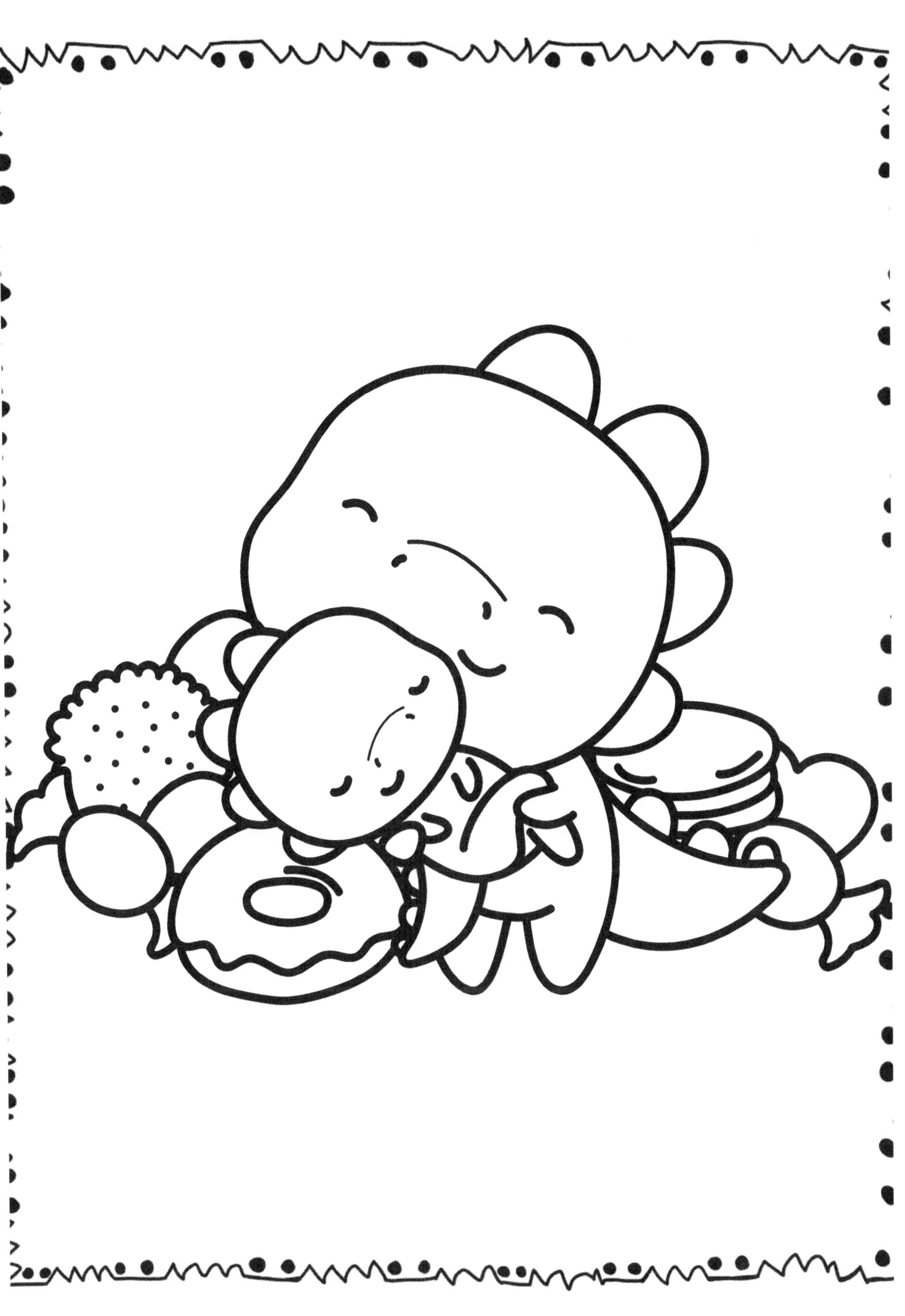

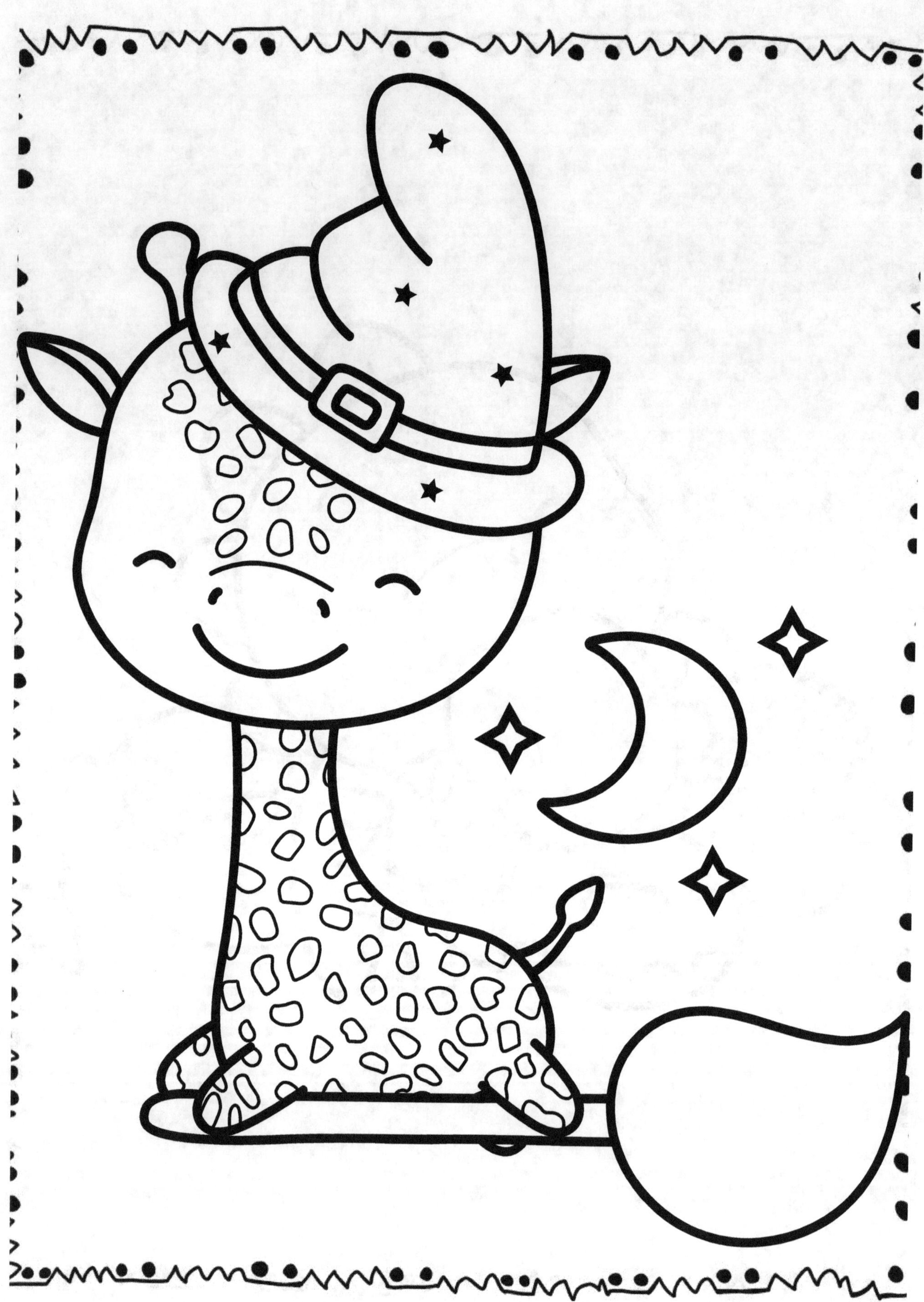

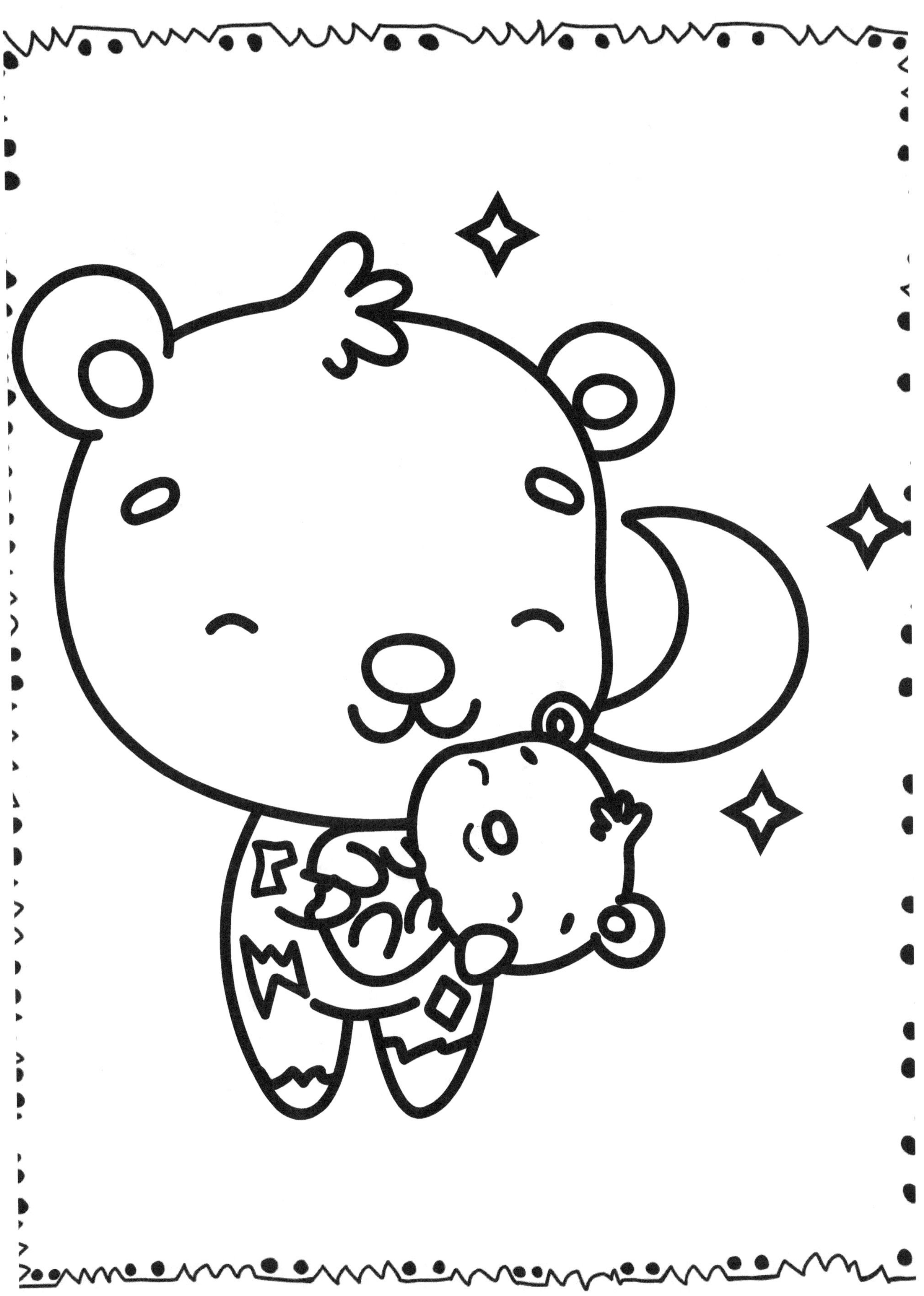

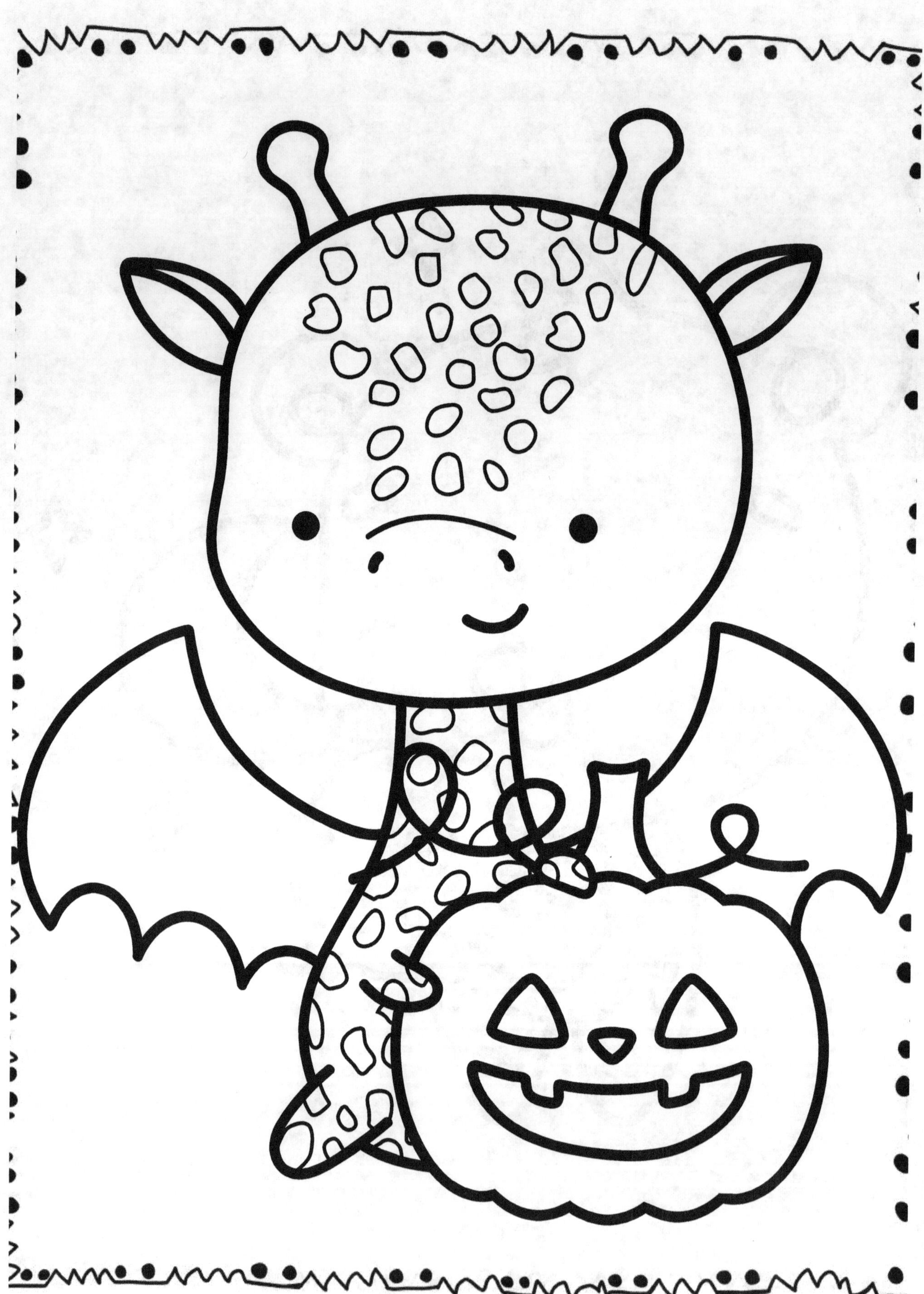

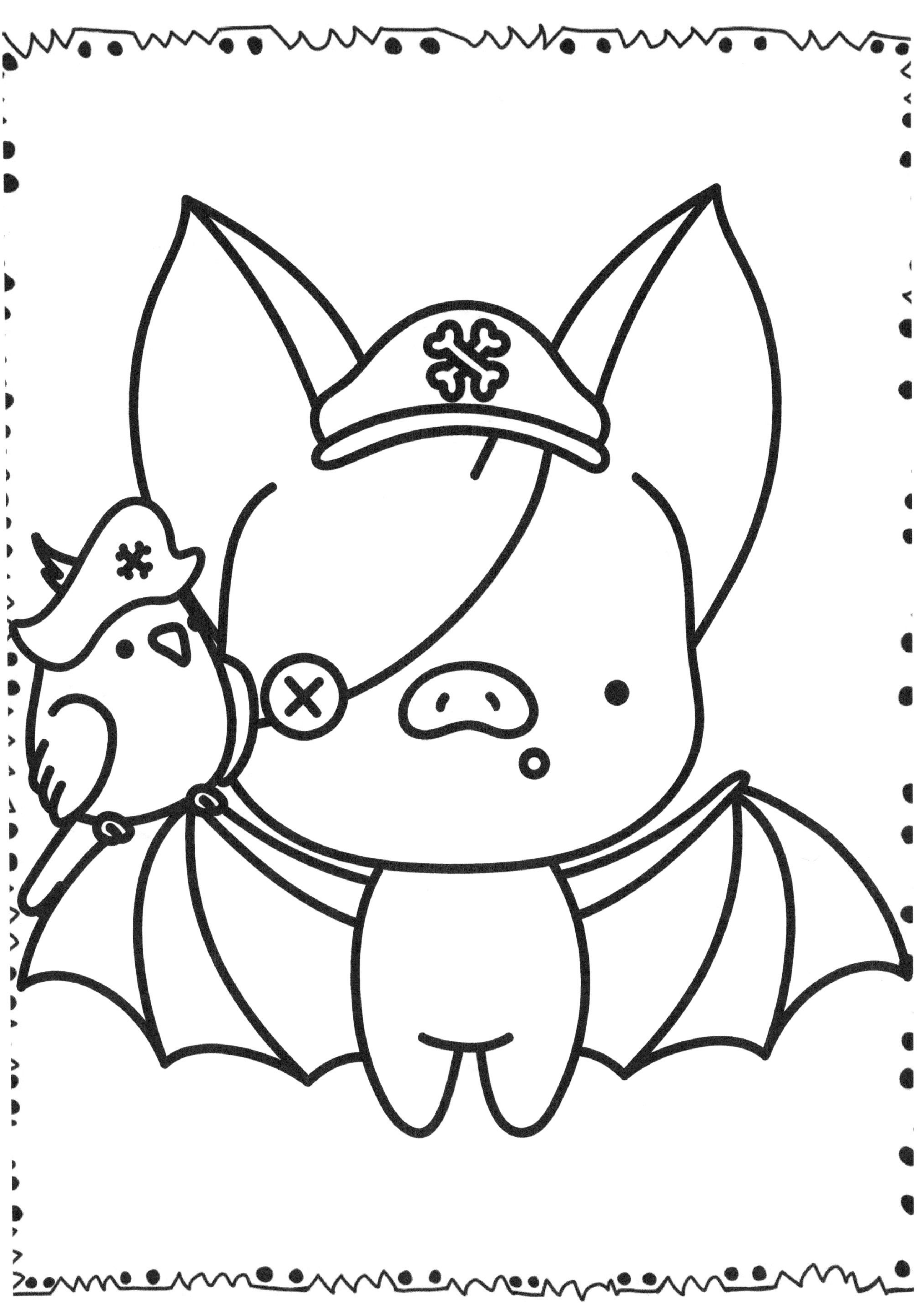

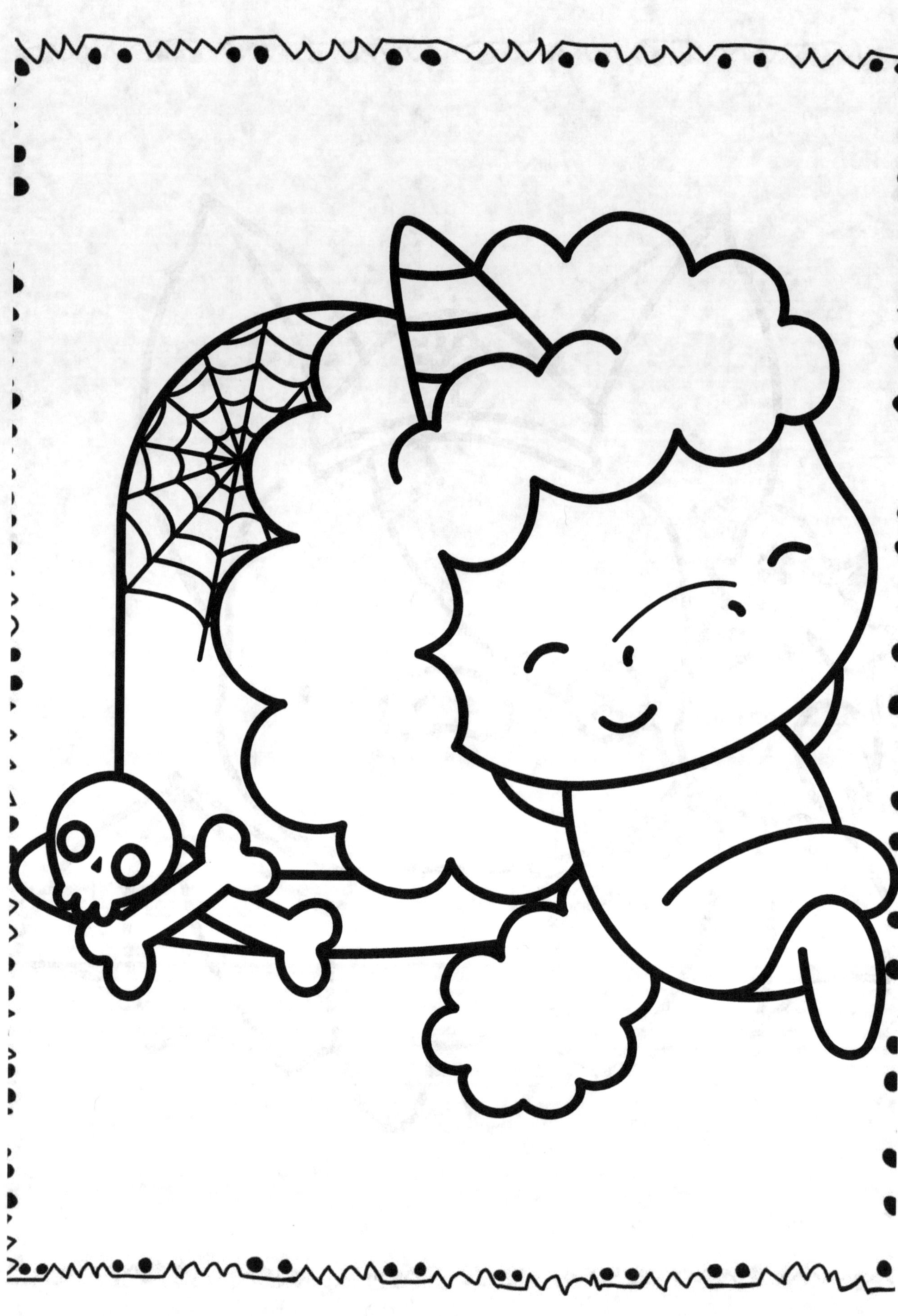